# Mary Magdalene: A Sanctuary of Remembrance

Rose Pocket Sanctuary Series™ – Volume II

"Where the mind is, there is the treasure."

— *The Gospel of Mary.*

Mary Magdalene: A Sanctuary of Remembrance
Rose Pocket Sanctuary Series – Volume II

This Pocket Sanctuary is intended for personal spiritual enrichment and reflection. It is not meant to replace professional, medical, or therapeutic guidance.

Published by Rooted Hound Press
Vienna, New Jersey
rootedhoundpress.com

Cover design by Rooted Hound Press.

ISBN 978-1-969687-08-2

Printed in the United States of America.

First Edition: 2025

# The Rose Series™ – Pocket Sanctuaries

A devotional collection exploring the Rose Lineage, the feminine path of remembrance, and the quiet wisdom that awakens the soul.

**Volume I**
*The Rose Codex*
A guide to the ancient symbolism of the Rose and the heart-centered path of awakening.

**Volume II**
*Mary Magdalene: A Sanctuary of Remembrance*
A restoration of the Magdalene's voice, presence, and feminine wisdom.

**Volume III**

*The Magdalene Path*
An embodied guide to living the Rose teachings through daily devotion, truth, softness, and inner remembrance.

**Forthcoming Volumes**
*The Magdalene Path: Daily Practices*
*The Lost Feminine Gospels*
*The Rose Priestess*
*The Rose at the End of the World*
(Additional volumes will continue to unfold.)

*For the women who were rewritten,*
*misnamed, misplaced, or misunderstood—*
*and still remembered their truth.*
*For the ones who kept their wisdom alive*
*in silence, in softness, in devotion.*
*For every soul rediscovering its voice,*
*its power, its lineage,*
*and its right to rise.*
*This Sanctuary is for you.*

# Preface: Why Her Voice Matters Now

History rarely erases a woman because she is small. It erases her because she is radiant. Because she holds a truth that cannot be controlled. Because she stands close to something the world is not ready to honor.

Mary Magdalene's story was never lost — it was buried beneath sermons, translations, politics, and the long shadow of fear. Yet wherever truth is buried, it begins to rise again.

Today, her voice resurfaces not as a correction of the past but as a *remembrance* for the present.

She returns as:

- the healer
- the witness
- the teacher of inner authority
- the one who remained rooted when others fled
- the feminine face of devotion and clarity

This Sanctuary is not here to retell history. It is here to restore the *symbolic truth* of who she was —and who we become when we reclaim the exiled parts of ourselves.

Mary Magdalene rises now because the world is ready to listen.

# HOW TO USE THIS SANCTUARY

This Pocket Sanctuary is meant to be read slowly.

You do not need to complete it in one sitting. You do not need to take notes or "keep up." You do not need any prior knowledge of the Rose, Mary Magdalene, or spiritual symbolism.

Simply move at the pace that feels natural to you.

Each section offers:

## ✦ A Teaching

A gentle explanation of the Rose's wisdom and how it applies to your everyday life.

## ✦ An Affirmation

A sentence to anchor the lesson into your heart.

## ✦ A Journaling Prompt

A doorway for deeper inner exploration.

There is no right way to use this Sanctuary. You may:

> read one section a day
>
> move intuitively between pages

return to certain teachings when needed

use this as part of a morning ritual

keep it by your bedside

read it quietly with tea

tuck it into your bag as a reminder of your path

Let this Sanctuary be what it was designed to be:

A small companion. A gentle teacher. A reminder that your soul unfolds one petal at a time.

When you're ready, turn the page and enter the first teaching.

# Contents

# SECTION 1 — The Beloved of the Rose

*She comes in silence,*
*soft as breath upon stone,*
*carrying a lamp the world once hid.*
*Her hands smell of myrrh,*
*her robe of rose,*
*her eyes of a woman who remembers*
*what others tried to forget.*
*Beloved of the Beloved,*
*Keeper of the quiet truth—*
*Mary of the radiant heart,*
*we turn toward you now.*

There are women whose names survive through history, and then there are women whose truths survive despite it. Mary Magdalene is the latter. For centuries, her identity was fractured—misnamed, mislabeled, and rewritten to fit the fears and power structures of those who came after her. But truth has a way of resurfacing. Mary was not a fallen woman; she was a chosen woman. A witness. A teacher. A companion in the most profound spiritual sense. A bearer of the sacred oils. A keeper of mysteries. A woman trusted with knowledge that frightened men in power. She wasn't erased because she was insignificant—she was erased because she wasn't. And now, as the collective rises into a new era of intuitive knowing, her voice is returning—quiet but steady, like a memory in the soul you didn't know you carried. This sanctuary begins with the simplest truth: Mary Magdalene was beloved—by Jesus, by the early community, and by the lineage of the Rose that she carried long before her name was ever spoken. Her story opens not with sin, but with devotion. Not with shame, but with remembrance.

**Affirmation:**

"I reclaim what was forgotten. I honor the feminine wisdom that endures."

**Journaling Prompt:**

What beliefs about yourself have been shaped by someone else's story? And what part of you is ready to reclaim your true name?

# SECTION 2 — Keeper of the Anointing Oils

*She carries the scent of sanctity—*
*frankincense on her wrists, myrrh in her palms,*
*rose lingering like a memory on her breath.*
*Where she walks, the air softens.*
*Where she stands, the sacred gathers.*

Long before Mary Magdalene became a disciple, she was known for something older, quieter, and far more powerful: her mastery of the sacred oils. In ancient traditions, anointing was not simply fragrance—it was initiation. Oils were used to bless kings, soothe the dying, honor the sacred, and awaken the soul. The woman who held the oils was not a servant; she was a priestess. Scripture speaks little of her early life, but history outside the canon remembers her differently: as a healer, an herbalist, a woman trained in the mysteries of scent, plant medicine, and ritual preparation. When she anointed Jesus, she was performing a sacred act recognized in nearly every spiritual tradition of her time. It was not an act of submission, but of understanding. Oils were used for clearing the mind, grounding the spirit, opening the heart, and preparing one for initiation. Mary knew this. She brought the oils because she recognized the moment. She honored him the way a priestess honors a teacher: with devotion, understanding, and sacred skill. And in that moment, she revealed something crucial—Mary was not following from behind; she was moving in step with him, prepared for a path most others could not see. The woman who carries the oils is the woman who knows how to open what is closed, soothe what is wounded, and awaken what has been forgotten. She sees with her senses and teaches through presence. This section is a reminder that your healing gifts—whatever form they take—are not small. They are part of an ancient lineage of women who have always tended the sacred.

**Affirmation:**

"I carry healing in my hands, wisdom in my senses, and sacred remembrance in my breath."

**Journaling Prompt:**

Where do your natural healing abilities show up in your life—through your presence, your intuition, your touch, or your way of seeing others?

# SECTION 3 — Companion of the Light

*She walked beside the Teacher,*
*not behind him.*
*Not in shadow, not in secrecy—beside.*
*Light recognizes light.*
*Devotion recognizes devotion.*
*And wisdom knows its equal when it stands before it.*

Mary Magdalene was not a background figure. She was not a follower lost in the crowd. She was a companion—one who walked the path with clarity, presence, and spiritual understanding. The early texts describe her not as someone "rescued," but as someone who recognized the teachings instantly, as though remembering something she had always known. Some scholars refer to her as "the disciple who understood," and in many traditions she is seen as the one who grasped the spiritual message more deeply than the others. She was present at moments when others fled. She listened when others argued. She received teachings that others were not ready for. And she was entrusted with the most profound revelation of all: the message of the resurrection. She was the first to see him, the first to hear him, the first to carry the news. This is not the role of a minor character. This is the role of a companion—one who stands shoulder to shoulder with the Teacher, not to replace or overshadow, but to reflect, support, and illuminate. The early followers saw Mary at his side. Later traditions tried to move her behind him. But the truth remains: she was there in the center of the story, not the margins. In every spiritual journey, there are moments when we, too, are asked to step out of the shadows and stand beside the light of our own becoming. To stop diminishing ourselves. To stop assuming we are less than we are. The path asks us not only to follow—but eventually, to stand in our own radiance.

**Affirmation:**

"I walk in my own light, confident, steady, and seen."

**Journaling Prompt:**

In what areas of your life have you been standing behind others instead of beside them? And what would shift if you allowed yourself to stand fully in your own light?

# SECTION 4 — The Exiled Feminine

*Her name was rewritten,*
*her story reshaped,*
*her truth buried beneath the weight of centuries.*
*Yet the rose does not forget its bloom,*
*even when pressed between the pages of someone else's book.*

Mary Magdalene's story is one of the most powerful examples of what happens when feminine wisdom threatens the structures built to contain it. Across history, when women carried healing, intuition, or spiritual authority, they were often recast into roles that felt "safer" for the world around them—diminished, dismissed, or distorted. Mary was no exception. In the sixth century, a single sermon incorrectly labeled her a repentant prostitute, and that misunderstanding shaped global perception for more than a thousand years. Why? Because a woman who was a healer, a teacher, and a spiritual equal was more dangerous to the systems of her time than a woman who needed saving. Recasting her narrative made her easier to control—and easier to erase. But the truth has a long life. Today, her name is being restored by historians, theologians, and spiritual seekers who know that the feminine face of wisdom was never lost, only silenced. And in that restoration, we see a reflection of our own journey. How many parts of your inner feminine—your intuition, compassion, sensuality, emotional intelligence, healing presence—have been exiled, judged, or misunderstood? How often has your softness been mistaken for weakness, your power for threat, or your knowing for defiance? Mary's story reminds us that what is exiled can return, what is suppressed can rise, and what is misnamed can be renamed by the one it belongs to. The feminine was never broken—it was buried. And now it is remembering how to rise.

**Affirmation:**

"I reclaim the parts of myself that were silenced, shamed, or misunderstood."

**Journaling Prompt:**

What parts of your inner feminine have you hidden or minimized to feel safe or accepted? And which of those parts are ready to return?

# SECTION 5 — The Gospel of Mary

*Pages missing, lines torn away,*
*words scattered like petals in the wind—*
*yet what remains is enough.*
*A fragment of truth, a whisper of the sacred,*
*a gospel that survives*
*because the soul recognizes what cannot be erased.*

The Gospel of Mary is one of the most extraordinary spiritual texts ever discovered—not because it is complete, but because it survived at all. Found in fragments within the Berlin Codex and echoed in the Nag Hammadi Library, the gospel presents a side of early teachings that few people ever learned: Mary Magdalene was a teacher in her own right. In this gospel, she comforts the disciples when they are afraid. She explains the nature of the soul, the illusion of fear, and the path to inner peace. She speaks of the "powers" the soul must rise through—layers of ignorance, craving, wrath, and confusion—until it returns to clarity. She teaches that our true authority comes from within, not from external structures or titles. And in one of the most powerful moments, the Teacher tells Mary, "Blessed are you, that you did not waver at the sight of Me." This line alone reveals the depth of her understanding. The gospel also preserves a very human moment: Peter challenges her, doubting that the Teacher would reveal things to her that he did not reveal to them. Levi responds with a rebuke that has echoed through centuries: "Surely the Teacher loved her more than us." Whether "more" reflects affection, understanding, or spiritual readiness is not the point. The point is this: Mary was trusted. She received teachings others were not ready to hear. She carried wisdom others were uncomfortable acknowledging. And she held her ground even when her voice was questioned. The Gospel of Mary reminds us that the soul's authority does not come from approval—it comes from inner alignment. It teaches that insight arises from clarity, not hierarchy. And it invites us to rise through our own layers of fear and illusion to reclaim the truth already waiting within us.

**Affirmation:**

"I trust the wisdom that rises from within me, even when others do not understand it."

**Journaling Prompt:**

Where in your life have you doubted your own inner authority because someone else questioned it? And what truth is ready to be reclaimed as yours?

# SECTION 6 — The Teacher of Remembrance

*She does not give answers;*
*she awakens memory.*
*She does not command the path;*
*she reveals it within you.*
*Her teaching is not instruction—*
*it is remembrance.*

Mary Magdalene is often remembered not for what she taught, but for what she *reflected* to those around her: that the truth they sought was already within them. In the Gospel of Mary, she tells the disciples that fear blinds them, that the mind creates illusions, and that peace is found when the soul remembers what it truly is. This is not the teaching of a follower—it is the teaching of someone who has gone inward, descended into her own depths, and returned with clarity. Mary's wisdom arose from the same place all true spiritual insight comes from: inner remembrance. She understood that awakening is not about adding more—it is about removing what obscures the truth. She knew that fear makes the world feel solid and heavy, while love makes it transparent. She saw that the mind creates barriers, while the soul dissolves them. She understood that guidance is not control—it is companionship. And she lived this truth with extraordinary steadiness, even when those around her doubted her voice. Mary teaches us that spiritual awakening is not about becoming someone new. It is about remembering who we have always been. It is not about striving— it is about softening. Not about perfection—it is about presence.

The Teacher she followed awakened remembrance in her. And she, in turn, became a teacher of remembrance for others. You are not here to earn your worth. You are here to remember it.

**Affirmation:**

"I remember who I am beneath fear, beneath doubt, beneath every story ever placed upon me."

**Journaling Prompt:**

What truth about yourself have you forgotten, and what would your life feel like if you remembered it fully?

# SECTION 7 — Sacred Love as a Frequency

*Not the love that clings,*
*but the love that clears.*
*Not the love that demands,*
*but the love that awakens.*
*Not the love of longing,*
*but the love that remembers:*
*we are made of the same light.*

Few figures in spiritual history have been more misunderstood than Mary Magdalene—especially when it comes to the nature of her connection to Jesus. For centuries, people have debated whether they were partners, companions, spouses, or simply teacher and disciple. But when we strip away the projections and the fears of the early church, one truth remains: their relationship carried a frequency of sacred love. Sacred love is not romance, though it can include tenderness. It is not possession, though it can create deep belonging. It is not a hierarchy, though it recognizes wisdom. Sacred love is the frequency that rises when two souls recognize each other beyond the boundaries of fear, ego, identity, and story. It is the meeting of two beings who remember the divine spark within themselves—and therefore recognize it in the other. This is why Mary understood the teachings so quickly. Sacred love opens the inner senses. It softens resistance. It dissolves the illusions that keep us afraid of our own light. In the Gospel narratives, Mary is the one who remains when others flee, the one who listens without defensiveness, the one who sees without distortion. She perceives through the heart, not the mind. And when you perceive through the heart, everything becomes clearer. Sacred love elevates both people into truer versions of themselves. It does not diminish. It does not bind. It does not demand. It illuminates. This kind of love is not exclusive to great spiritual figures. It is available in every human connection where presence, truth, and soul-recognition exist. Mary teaches us that the highest love is not about ownership—it is about awakening. And the most significant spiritual relationships are those that help us see who we truly are.

**Affirmation:**

"I welcome relationships that awaken my soul, not diminish my light."

**Journaling Prompt:**

When have you experienced a connection—romantic or not—that felt like recognition rather than attachment? What did it reveal about who you truly are?

# SECTION 8 — The Rose Lineage

*The rose blooms in silence,*
*carrying ancient memory in every spiral.*
*A symbol of the hidden path,*
*the open heart, the wisdom*
*that survives in fragrance*
*long after the petals fall.*

Long before Mary Magdalene walked the desert paths of Galilee, the rose was already a sacred symbol. It represented the mysteries of the feminine, the unfolding of consciousness, and the quiet strength held in beauty. In many ancient traditions, priestesses, healers, and keepers of intuitive wisdom were associated with the rose. Temple lineages in Egypt, Sumer, Greece, and the Levant used the rose to symbolize inner initiation—movements of the heart that could not be taught through doctrine, only through experience. When Mary appears in later spiritual texts surrounded by rose imagery, it is not accidental. It is memory. She carried the qualities the rose embodied: devotion, inner knowing, patience, courage, softness with strength woven through it. The spiral at the center of the rose mirrors the journey of remembrance—returning again and again to more profound truth, not in a straight line, but in a widening circle. The rose teaches that awakening does not happen all at once. It unfolds. Petal by petal, truth opens. Layer by layer, old identities fall away. And at the center lies the heart— unprotected, unguarded, luminous. Mary Magdalene belongs to what many call the Rose Lineage: a stream of women and men throughout history who carried the frequency of the awakened heart. Not a religion, but a remembering. Not a doctrine, but a presence. Not a hierarchy, but a resonance. To belong to the Rose Lineage is to honor the sacred through gentleness, to lead through integrity, to heal through compassion, to teach through lived experience. It is to walk the world with an open heart—even when the world does not understand it. And it is to trust the timeless truth that what is grown in the heart endures, even when the world tries to bury it.

**Affirmation:**

"I am part of a lineage of love, healing, and conscious awakening."

**Journaling Prompt:**

In your own life, where do you feel the "rose" unfolding—slowly revealing deeper layers of who you are becoming?

# SECTION 9 — The Path of Devotion

*Devotion is not kneeling; it is opening.*
*Not obedience; but presence.*
*Not the giving away of your power,*
*but the remembering of where it truly comes from.*

Mary Magdalene's devotion has often been misunderstood. People have mistaken it for submission, sentimentality, or emotional dependence. But devotion, in its most valid spiritual form, is not about diminishing oneself. It is about aligning oneself. Devotion is the steady return to what is true, even when fear tries to scatter the mind. It is the willingness to stay present when others run, to listen when others argue, to soften when others harden. Mary embodied this. Her devotion was the expression of clarity, not confusion. It allowed her to stand at the foot of the cross when everyone else fled. It allowed her to approach the tomb alone, guided by love rather than fear. It allowed her to recognize the Teacher in a moment when even grief clouded her sight. And it allowed her to carry the message of resurrection with unwavering strength. True devotion is not a loss of self—it is the anchoring of self. It is the heart's ability to remain open in moments that would normally close it. It is the soul's ability to recognize truth beyond appearance. Devotion is what roots you when the world moves. It is what steadies you when doubt rises. It is what keeps your heart alive when circumstances try to numb it. In your own life, devotion does not need to take the form of ritual or ceremony. It can be the devotion to your healing, your peace, your inner truth. It can be the devotion to honesty, integrity, compassion, or joy. It can be the devotion to your spiritual path—even when you feel you are walking it alone. Mary teaches that devotion is not about perfection, but about presence. It is the practice of returning, again and again, to what matters most.

**Affirmation:**

"My devotion strengthens me. What I return to, I become."

**Journaling Prompt:**

What are you devoted to—not in obligation, but in love? And how does that devotion shape who you are becoming?

# SECTION 10 — Your Own Rose Gospel

*Your life is a scripture*
*written in breath and becoming.*
*Every truth you reclaim is a verse.*
*Every healing you embody is a chapter.*
*Every step toward wholeness is a line that only you could write.*

The Gospel of Mary survived in fragments—missing pages, torn lines, gaps where someone once tried to silence her voice. And yet, what remained was enough to reveal her strength, her clarity, her devotion, and her wisdom. Your life is not so different. There are parts of your story that feel missing, parts that were misunderstood, and parts that were reshaped by others who did not fully see you. There may be chapters you wish you could rewrite, and moments you wish had never been written at all. But the truth is this: you are still here. Your soul is still speaking. And the gospel of your life—the truth of who you are—is still unfolding. Mary Magdalene did not wait for permission to speak her truth. She did not wait for validation from those who doubted her. She trusted the wisdom that rose within her, even when others questioned it. And she continued to walk her path with courage. You are invited to do the same. Your inner gospel is the collection of truths you have learned through experience, intuition, resilience, and grace. It is shaped not by perfection, but by presence. Not by certainty, but by willingness. Not by what you were told, but by what you *remember*. And as you walk forward—through healing, awakening, undoing, rebuilding—you are writing the next chapter. One choice at a time. One truth at a time. One return to your own

19

heart at a time. Let this sanctuary remind you that your voice matters. Your story matters. And the wisdom blooming within you is part of a lineage that cannot be erased.

**Affirmation:**

"I am the author of my becoming. My truth is worthy. My voice is rising."

**Journaling Prompt:**

If you were to write the first line of your own "gospel"—the truth your soul most wants to speak—what would it be?

# SECTION 11 — The Woman Who Stayed

*She did not flee,*
*though the world shook.*
*She did not harden,*
*though grief pressed in.*
*She stayed—not because she was unafraid,*
*but because love anchored her feet*
*where courage called her to stand.*

One of the most overlooked truths about Mary Magdalene is also one of the simplest: **She stayed.** When others fled — out of fear, shock, or despair — she remained present. At the cross, at the tomb, in the early community, in the silence after great loss. She stayed where love guided her, not where fear permitted her.

Mary's endurance was not passive. It was fierce. Rooted. A form of spiritual strength that comes from knowing the truth in your bones. Her story teaches us that staying — with grief, with truth, with ourselves — can be a radical act of devotion.

Sometimes the most sacred courage is not moving at all, but remaining open in places that once broke us.

**Affirmation:**

"I have the courage to stay present with what matters."

**Journaling Prompt:**

Where in your life have you remained present, even when it was hard — and what did that endurance reveal about your heart?

# Closing Blessing

May the wisdom of the Rose guard your heart.
May the remembrance of Mary guide your steps.
May the truth you reclaim root itself gently within you.
May every forgotten part of you return home.
May you walk with the steadiness of one who knows they are
loved, the courage of one who knows they are guided,
and the softness of one who trusts their own unfolding.
May the sacred rise in you—not as noise, but as knowing.
Not as striving, but as presence.
Not as pressure, but as peace.
And as you move forward from this sanctuary,
May you carry the assurance that your light is needed,
Your voice is blessed,
and your becoming is holy.
Go with remembrance.
Go with gentleness.
Go with the Rose at your heart.

# PUBLICATIONS BY ROOTED HOUND PRESS

### The Rose Series™ — Pocket Sanctuaries
*The Rose Codex*
*Mary Magdalene: A Sanctuary of Remembrance*
*The Magdalene Path*
(Additional titles forthcoming)

### Pocket Sanctuary Series™
*Whispers from the Soul*
*The Test That I Refused*
(Future mini-sanctuaries coming soon)

### Books by Rooted Hound Press
*Returning to Wholeness: An Invitation to the Soul*
*Echoes Through the Spiral: A Soul's Continuum*
*Healing the Past Through the Present*
*Encoded in Stone: The Memory of Earth & The Story of Us*
*Thoth & the Tablets: A Journey Through the Crystalline Codes*
*The Adventures of Layla and Lilly* (Children's Series)

### Journals & Companions
*Rooted Reflections Journal*
*The Rose Journal*
*Celestial Journal*
*Floral Journal*
(Additional themed journals coming soon)

Published by
Rooted Hound Press
Vienna, New Jersey
**www.rootedhoundpress.com**

www.ingramcontent.com/pod-product-compliance
Lightning Source LLC
Chambersburg PA
CBHW070050040426
42331CB00034B/2966